Temeka's Choice

Temeka Johnson

Illustrated by Lynda Farrington Wilson

Temeka's Choice

H.O.P.E. Foundation

Illustrated by Lynda Farrington Wilson
www.lyndafarringtonwilson.com

ISBN 978-0615627137

Foreword

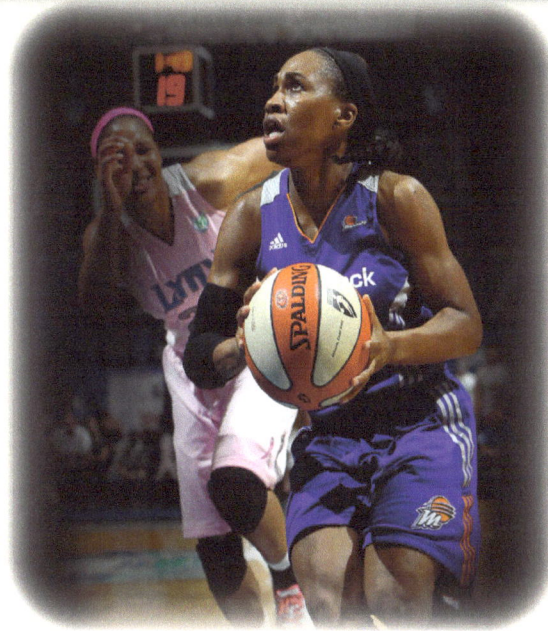

TEMEKA JOHNSON

... has always had a passion for giving back. Through the H.O.P.E. Foundation, she is able to do so and is very excited about sharing her stories and experiences. From a little girl playing in the streets with the boys, to becoming a WNBA Champion, Temeka talks about where it all begins.
This is where Temeka's Choice, a twist from her first book, "Meeks Moments" comes in. This series will highlight the many challenges that she had to endure while on her journey to becoming who she is today.

I hope that you enjoy reading this book, because I surely enjoyed writing it.

Special Thanks

To God, Jewel Johnson-Mae, Veronica Johnson (Mother), Eric Johnson, To all my family and close friends (you know who you are), John Walsh, Alex Chambers (For all your help and guidance), Bob Starkey, Shirley Campbell (For being there from the beginning), River Ridge (where it all begin), Kenner Louisiana (Will always be my home) and last but not least, to all my fans...
I appreciate all of your support and know that it will continue.

Dedication

IN LOVING MEMORY OF JEWEL JOHNSON...

...who was a great woman, mother, sister, teacher and friend.
Lovingly referred to by many as Ms. Mae, she was also well known
for the love that she poured out to the people around her.
Ms. Mae helped transform Temeka into the woman that she is
today starting at a very young age. Without her guidance
Temeka is not sure where she would have been.

Temeka thanks God everyday for blessing her with such a wonderful
grandmother for as long as He did, and for giving her
another Angel to watch over her.

Grandma Mae is loved and missed everyday.

Basketball was all that Temeka could ever think about. While other little girls were brushing the hair of a favorite doll or outside jumping double-dutch, Temeka was playing in a gym surrounded by the sounds of pounding basketballs and squeaking sneakers on the hardwood floor.

Temeka lived with her grandma, whom everyone called Mae. Temeka was very close to her family, but it was her Grandma Mae who knew her better than anyone else.

"Baby girl, you goin' to play ball with your friends after school today?" asked Mae.

"Yes, I am. You know there's nothin' better," Temeka replied.

"Well then, make sure. . . ."

"I know the rules," Temeka interrupted. "Be in the house before the streetlights come on; clean my room; and make sure my homework is done before I go to bed."

"Good. I don't need to remind you then," Mae said.

Those were the rules Temeka knew all too well. Sometimes she would forget them, but somehow she always managed to slide by. Nothing got between her and playing basketball.

Temeka played almost every day. She played basketball with her friends at recess and would even jump into a game at someone's house on her walk home from the bus stop. Temeka's uncles and cousins liked to play basketball too and often had an afternoon game going at her house.

"You wanna play ball with us?" her uncle asked.

"Can I?" squealed Temeka.

"Alright, but no cryin', okay? You start cryin' and we can't let you play with us," her uncle replied.

Mustering up all her courage, she said, "Okay, no cryin'. Deal." Temeka held her hand out to her uncle, who quickly gave it a firm shake.

"Alright then," he replied.

The game was rough. A few times Temeka took a hit or a shove. She wanted to cry but held back the tears. As long as she got to play, a few extra scrapes were worth it.

The more Temeka played with her uncles and cousins, the better she became. With each game she got faster and stronger. She was a young girl, but Temeka had the courage to play just about anyone.

At school Temeka always played her best to make sure her team won. Her coach knew how good she was, so she taught Temeka to work with the other players who needed more practice.

"Come on, Coach," whined Temeka. "Do I have to?"

"Temeka, we know that you're a very good player, but wouldn't it be nice if you could share what you know about basketball?"

"Umm, I guess."

"'You guess? Temeka, what have I always told you?"

"'Players don't win championships. Teams do.'"

"That's right. Besides, you know that a lot of your teammates look up to you."

"I know. I always do my best, Coach."

Well, now you can do your best by helping your teammates to do their best. Tomorrow at practice you can be my assistant coach."

Temeka liked the sound of that. She began to imagine what would happen if everyone on the team could play as well as she did.

Unfortunately, any time she was thinking about basketball, she wasn't thinking of much else, such as schoolwork or the rules she was supposed to follow.

Walking home from school one day, Temeka saw a group of boys playing in the street, and she couldn't resist dropping her book bag and joining in.

"What's up, shorty?" a tall boy asked as he looked up from the game that had come to a stop. It was Brandon, a boy new to the neighborhood. "Uh, you gonna watch us play?" He chuckled.

"No, I wanna play," Temeka replied.

"Ha!" Brandon laughed. "Girls can't play no ball!"

Temeka had heard boys say things like that before. At recess sometimes the boys would not let her play, telling her that girls weren't any good at basketball.

"C'mon man," one of the other boys chimed in. "This is Temeka. She's good. Now we'll have enough to play three on three."

"Well, all right," said Brandon as he stretched and yawned. "I'm a little tired, so I guess I won't have to try too hard anyway."

Temeka didn't say a word. The other boys knew that she played at home against her uncles and cousins, who were much bigger and tougher than they were. Brandon had no idea.

When Temeka made a basket, Brandon would say,
"Beginner's luck," or "We're goin' easy on you because you're a girl."
After a while it seemed as though the game was between
only her and Brandon, as though the other boys weren't even there.

Before they knew it, the score was tied. Whoever made the next
basket would win. Temeka had the ball, and with a quick move she
flew by Brandon, charged toward the basket, and stopped for a jump
shot. Brandon tried to slap the ball away but instead hit Temeka's
arm. The ball bounced off the rim and landed in a nearby yard.

"That was a foul!" shouted Temeka.

"Stop your whining. That wasn't no foul!" Brandon yelled.
"I told you already. Girls can't play ball!"

All Temeka could do was to frown and stare at the hoop.
She tucked the basketball behind her hip and thought to herself,
I'm going to finish this game!

Just then a loud voice called out from down the street. "Braaaaaaandon!"

"Aw man. That's my mom. I gotta go," Brandon griped as he began running down the street.

Temeka looked up to see that the streetlights had just come on. She stood watching all the other boys running at full speed down the street.

Then she heard her grandma's voice, "Temeeeeeeeka!"
She knew she was going to be in trouble when she got home.

Temeka flew through the door, ran past her grandma, waved, and quickly said, "Hi!"

"Temeka, you get back here right now," her grandmother demanded. "You had me so worried! You know you're supposed to be home before those streetlights come on."

"But Mae, I was just playing basketball down the street. This new boy, Brandon, was being mean, sayin' I couldn't play."

"You know better. I think if you don't get to play basketball tomorrow, then maybe you'll remember next time."

"But Mae. . . ."

"Don't 'But Mae' me! You keep this up and there'll be no basketball all week."

"But tomorrow is the last game before the big championship next week. My team needs me!"

"Then maybe next time you'll make the right choice and follow the rules."

Temeka fought back tears, just as she had done before on the basketball court. She stomped off to her room, threw down her book bag, slammed the door, and dove face first onto her bed.
"When I'm grown, I'll play basketball anytime I want," she mumbled to herself.

Later that night Temeka dreamed of the day when she would make that shot against Brandon and show him how good she was.

The next morning Temeka came into the kitchen ready for school. Grandma Mae had her breakfast ready—scrambled eggs, grits, and toast. She sat at the table sipping a cup of coffee while Temeka stared down at her food as she ate.

"Are you gonna stay mad at me forever?" her grandmother said with a smile.

"I guess not," muttered Temeka.

"That's good. Now eat your breakfast and get yourself to the bus stop."

"Mae?" asked Temeka. "Why do kids always have to follow the rules that adults set?"

"Baby girl, you learn to follow the rules when you're young. When you're old enough," she continued, "that's when you can make rules for yourself."

"When will I be old enough? I can't wait! I'll make the rule that I can play basketball whenever I want."

"Hold on there, child. You got a long way to go," said Mae. "You have to start making better choices first. You need to learn why we have rules."

"What kind of choices?" asked Temeka.

"Just focus on what you're supposed to do and make the choice you know is right."

Temeka looked back with a smile and nodded. "Okay," she agreed. As she left for school, Temeka was no longer mad at her grandma.

At recess Temeka could only watch her friends play basketball. Her grandmother knew all of Temeka's teachers, and they would tell her if Temeka played basketball when she wasn't supposed to.

After school Temeka sat on the bench and watched her team lose its first game of the season.

"Aww man!" said one of her teammates. "Can't believe we lost. Temeka, when are you comin' back?"

"I'll be back next week for the championship game. Don't you worry."

After the game Temeka walked over to her coach and asked whether she could practice for a little while.

"I thought Ms. Mae said you couldn't play today?" her coach replied.

"Uhh, well, I'm not really playing if it's just me," Temeka said with a grin. "C'mon, Coach. It's only practice."

"Okay, but if you get me in trouble with Ms. Mae, you're gonna have to answer for it. You have exactly one hour before I leave. Better make it worth your while."

"Oh, I will, Coach, I will!" Temeka shouted.

Temeka grabbed a basketball and started dribbling, then jumping and shooting the ball. She didn't even stop to catch her breath because she wanted to spend every second she had with a basketball in her hand.

On the way home from school Temeka felt tired, but that didn't bother her because she knew she was going to get to play basketball in the championship game.

"Well, well," a voice called from down the street. Brandon was shooting hoops by himself in his driveway. "You wanna try to finish that game?"

"Na, I . . . I gotta get home."

"Yeah, that's right." Brandon began egging her on. "I knew you'd give up."

Temeka threw down her book bag. "Gimme the ball!" she demanded.

Brandon bounced the ball her way. Temeka looked at it in her hands, then glared at Brandon. She noticed that it was getting dark and knew it wouldn't be long before the streetlights came on.

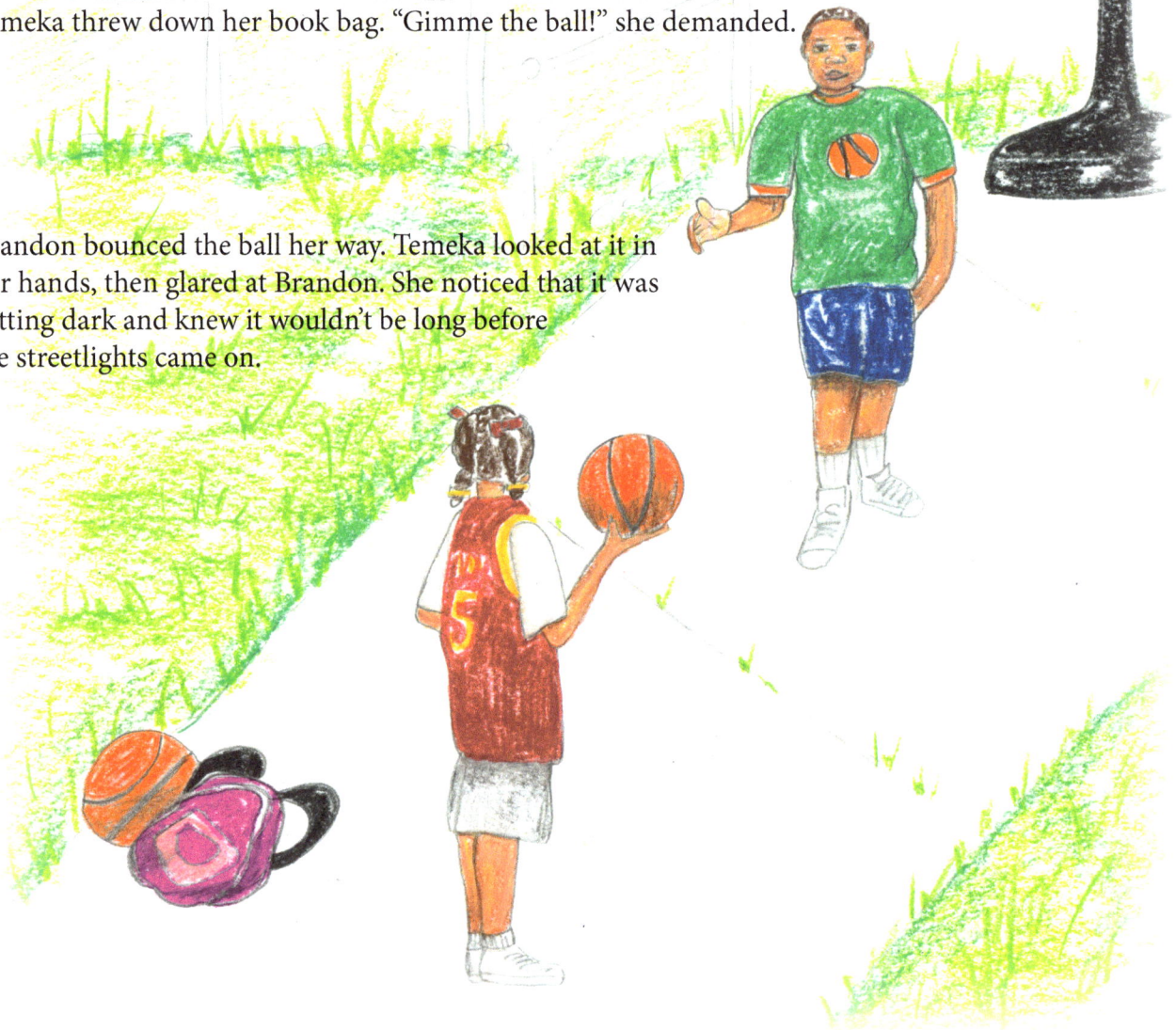

Just then she heard Grandma Mae's voice echo in her mind: "Just focus on what you're supposed to do and make the choice you know is right."

Temeka quickly bounced the ball back to Brandon. "Na, another time. I got a more important game next week, and I'm not going to miss it because of you."

Before Brandon could say anything, Temeka grabbed her book bag and started running home as fast as she could. As she came up the front steps of her house, she saw the streetlights flicker and then glow. All she could do was smile.

The next week Temeka was ready for the big championship game. She was so excited that she could hardly hold still before the game started. When it began, Temeka ran up and down the court, calling the shots and making the plays. When the final buzzer went off, her team had won the championship. Temeka and her team gathered around the trophy at center court. Her uncle was there taking pictures of his jubilant niece.

Her teammates began meeting up with their families and getting ready to go home. While Temeka was gathering her things, she saw Brandon standing by the door.

"Well, I guess you're good," he said softly, staring at the floor. "I mean, your team won and all."

"Um," Temeka replied. "Thanks, I guess."

"Maybe we can finish that game some time?" Brandon suggested.

"Yeah, we can. You just tell me when," Temeka said with a smirk, "and no fouls this time."

Later that afternoon Temeka was practicing out in the driveway by herself. She was far too excited after the championship game to do anything else.

"Baby girl," Mae called from the front door. "How much longer are you going to be out there? You need to come in here and eat."

"I'll be in, Mae, as soon as the streetlights come on, I promise. I've learned my lesson."

"Oh, you did, did you?" Mae asked as she strolled out to the driveway.

"Yes ma'am," Temeka replied. "I'll never stay out after the streetlights come on again."

"I'm proud of you Temeka," said Mae. "I just hope you keep on learning lessons."

Temeka turned to her grandma and asked, "What do you mean? I gotta learn more lessons?"

"That's what life is. You're always learning lessons. Some lessons are easy, and some—well, like the one that kept you from playing basketball—aren't so easy."

"You mean I might not get to play basketball again?" asked Temeka.

"Only if you don't remember what you learned," said. Mae. "The more you learn now, the better grown-up you'll be. But you'll never stop learning."

"Well, I hope I don't have to learn any more lessons for a while. All I want to do now is play some basketball," replied Temeka.

Just then the streetlights came on.

"Aww, I wanted to make one last shot," Temeka griped.

"How about I play you for it?" asked Mae.

"Play me for it? C'mon, Grandma, You mean it?"

"Toss me the ball," Mae said. "If I make the shot, you have to go inside. If I don't, you can stay out and play as long as you like."

"Okay," Temeka shouted. "Best get ready, Mae. You're playin' a champion now!"

Temeka hadn't known that her grandma played basketball. For her it was a wonderful surprise.

This would be the best game of basketball she would ever get to play.

hope
HEAVEN OPENS PEOPLE'S EYES

Foundation for Temeka Johnson

Spreading HOPE • Inspiring Youth • Fostering Community

Founded in 2008, the H.O.P.E. Foundation's mission is to provide inspiration to youth, families and communities to help them lead a more emotionally healthy lifestyle. HOPE will provide the tools necessary to increase self esteem, physical activity and a unified community spirit.

HOPE has three main objectives for the foundation:

- To create an impactful presence in every community that Ms. Johnson adopts.
- To highlight the importance of education and funding for at-risk schools.
- To gain awareness for the initiatives and programs that HOPE provides for the communities that it serves.

HOPE Programs

Jewel Johnson Teacher Scholarship Fund

Annual scholarship helps send aspiring educators to a 4-yr institution. The scholarship is funded through donations and proceeds from the sales of Meek's books.

Adopt-a-School Program

HOPE searches for schools in need of various forms of assistance. Through donations and support, the foundation provides schools with the tools to better aide our students and teachers.

Father/Daughter Basketball Clinics

These special sponsored clinics engage fathers and daughters in a unique clinic experience led by Temeka that is sure to strengthen the bond between father and daughter.

Holiday HOPE

Another sponsored event, the foundation spreads holiday cheer by helping to feed families for the Holiday Season.

"We build programs based on community needs" - Temeka Johnson

www.temekajohnson.com